This Journal Belongs To:

_____

_____

_____

Nature Exploring
Tips & Tricks

(RULE #1, DON'T GET BITTEN BY A TICK. JUST KIDDING...BUT IT RHYMES)

Hi There!

If you're holding this book, then you must love nature and adventures. And this nature field journal will help you appreciate nature even more.

A good nature adventure engages all your senses.

We most often use our eyes, when out in nature. And we see amazing things: *the colorful fall leaves, the beautiful patterns on butterfly wings, the changing iridescent colors on the neck feathers of a male duck, or the colors of tiny wildflowers.*

But to be a true nature explorer, you have to use all your senses.

What are the sounds you hear? The more you listen the more you'll hear:
Leaves crunching under your feet.
The buzzing of flying insects.
A woodpecker drilling tirelessly for insects.
The sound of running water from a nearby stream.
The drip drop of melting snow.
Bird songs.
Scuttling rodents in the bush.
Rustling of leaves overhead. The sound of wind blowing.

And you'll also hear different sounds depending on where you are exploring – woods, open fields, mountain, near a river, by the ocean.

Don't forget to use your sense of smell when out in nature. Smells can tell us a lot about what is happening in nature at the moment: *the smell of young grass in the spring, the smell of blooming flowers, the smell of rotting leaves in the fall.*

Touch is also a great way to explore nature: *Rough bark, smooth grass, velvety leaves, cool stones.* But there are also things that you don't want to touch like *poison ivy and nettle* (depending on where you live). Nature is tricky like that, but that's what we love about it.

The one sense you should be weary of using on your nature adventures is taste. Best not to eat what you don't know, like mushrooms, berries or other fruit. Better to leave them for the animals.

To get you started, here are some cool things to look (and listen) for when exploring:

Birds of prey	Song birds	Mammals	Reptiles
Amphibians	Poisonous plants	Fish	Colorful birds
Woodpeckers	Berries	Fruits	Crawling insects
Flying insects	Turtles	Water birds	Butterflies
Fruiting plants	Pollinators	Moths	Caterpillars
Flowers	Animal tracks	Mushrooms	Snails
Earthworms	Nuts	Evidence of animals	Different leaves

You may not always see animals on your walks, but there is plenty of evidence that they are around.

 See how many animal clues you can spot next time you are outside:

Tracks	Eaten nuts and acorns	Holes in the ground	Chewed bark on trees
Sounds	Droppings	Holes in trees	Feathers
Shells	Earth mounds with holes	Fur tufts	Nests

Here is another fun game to play when outside. This time with nature sounds:

 Every time you're exploring try to "collect" as many sounds as possible. Make a list in your field log. Here are some examples:

BIRD SONG	WOODPECKER	SOUND OF WIND BLOWING
RUSTLING LEAVES	BUZZING INSECTS	ANIMAL CALLS
SOUNDS OF WATER	BIRD LANDING IN WATER	FISH SPLASHING IN WATER
BIRD CALLS	CRUNCHING LEAVES	WATER BIRD DIVING
YOUR FOOTSTEPS	SWAYING GRASS	FARM ANIMALS

When you are out in nature, always be on a sensory scavenger hunt.

So, get ready for your adventure, and don't forget to be prepared:

- ◯ Sturdy shoes
- ◯ Hat
- ◯ Backpack
- ◯ Water & snack
- ◯ Bug spray
- ◯ A nature log (this book)
- ◯ Something to write with
- ◯ Jacket (even in summer)
- ◯ Bags for collecting things
- ◯ Binoculars/camera

Nature
Scavenger Hunts

The Nature Explorer's Scavenger Hunt Song

Something thin, something tall,
Something big, something small.

Something young, something old,
Something that prefers the cold.

Something buzzing, flapping wings,
Far away a songbird sings.

Turtles basking, fishes swim,
Something that is always green.

Something you can take back home,
Something better left alone.

Something smooth, something rough,
Something stuck to your pant cuff.

Something making a loud sound,
Another falls softly to the ground.

Something rustles in the bush,
Something heard when people hush.

Something creepy, something crawly,
Something that is smooth and rolly.

Sticks and rocks, and jumping frogs,
Vernal pools and muddy bogs.

Something wet, something dry,
Something that can make you cry.

Something carried by the wind,
Something that will make you scream.

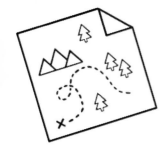

Something slimy, something shiny,
Something red and something grimy.

These and more you'll find outside,
Go exploring far and wide!

Spring Nature Scavenger Hunt

○ Bird on a branch	○ Crawling insect	○ Spider web
○ Frog or frog call	○ Budding leaves	○ Soaring bird
○ Human mud tracks	○ Flying insect	○ Nest
○ Water bird	○ Flowers	○ Fish

Design and draw your own **spring** nature scavenger hunt for your next adventure:

. . . .

○	○	○
○	○	○
○	○	○
○	○	○

Summer Nature Scavenger Hunt

○ Butterfly	○ Broad leaf	○ Flying insect
○ Spider	○ Turtle	○ Narrow, long leaf
○ Berries	○ Ladybug	○ Water bird
○ Fish	○ Soaring bird	○ Beetle

Design and draw your own **summer** nature scavenger hunt for your next adventure:

. . . .

○	○	○
○	○	○
○	○	○
○	○	○

Fall Nature Scavenger Hunt

Design and draw your own fall nature scavenger hunt for your next adventure:

. . . .

○	○	○
○	○	○
○	○	○
○	○	○

Winter Nature Scavenger Hunt

Design and draw your own **winter** nature scavenger hunt for your next adventure:

. . . .

○	○	○
○	○	○
○	○	○
○	○	○

Design and draw your own nature scavenger hunt for your next adventure:

. . . .

Design and draw your own nature scavenger hunt for your next adventure:

. . . .

Design and draw your own nature scavenger hunt for your next adventure:

. . . .

Nature Logs
&
Field Notes

Give this trip a name: _____

Place : _____ Date: _____ Season: _____

○ 🧗 **Hike**   ○ 🚲 **Bike**   ○ ⬜ **Other**
(DRAW YOUR OWN ADVENTURE ICON)

Water body visited on this trip:

○ RIVER/CANAL   ○ LAKE   ○ STREAM   ○ SEA/OCEAN

Who's with me: _____

What's the weather: ☀️ ☁️ 🌧️ 🌬️☁️ ❄️

If this nature outing had a badge, it would look like this:

Top 3 most interesting things I saw on this trip:

My sounds collection for this outing:

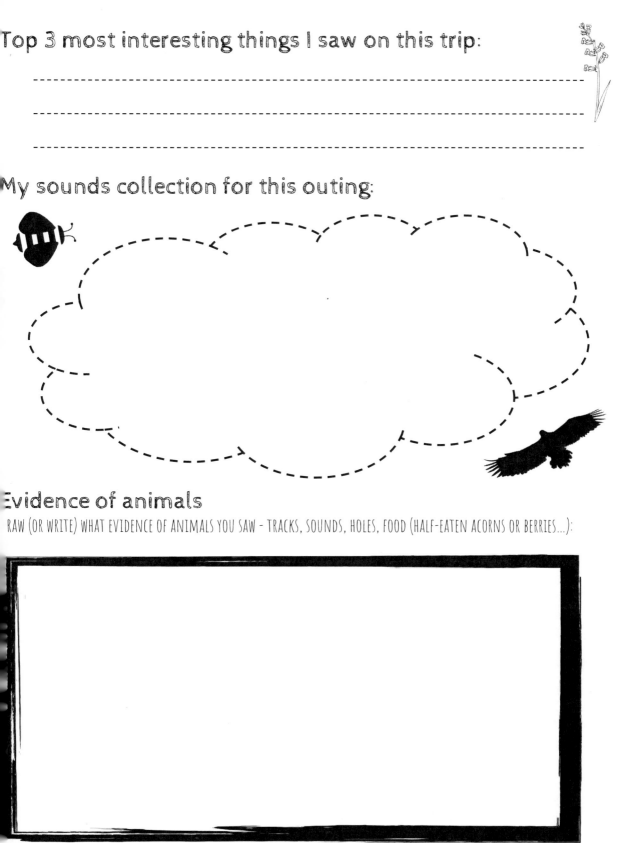

Evidence of animals

DRAW (OR WRITE) WHAT EVIDENCE OF ANIMALS YOU SAW - TRACKS, SOUNDS, HOLES, FOOD (HALF-EATEN ACORNS OR BERRIES...):

Nature Adventure #2

Give this trip a name: _____

Place : _____ Date: _____ Season: _____

○ 🧗 **Hike**   ○ 🚲 **Bike**   ○ [ ] **Other**
(DRAW YOUR OWN ADVENTURE ICON)

Water body visited on this trip:

○ RIVER/CANAL   ○ LAKE   ○ STREAM   ○ SEA/OCEAN

Who's with me: _____

What's the weather: ☀   ☁   🌧   🌬☁   ❄

My sounds, smells and textures collection for this trip:
(LIST OR DRAW ALL THE COOL THINGS YOU HEARD, SMELLED OR TOUCHED ON THIS ADVENTURE)

What is nature doing at this time of the year? What part of their life cycle are plants, insects, birds and other animals in?

Draw the most interesting plants, insects, birds and other animals you saw on this trip:

Give this trip a name: _____

Place : _____ Date: _____ Season: _____

○ 🧗 Hike   ○ 🚲 Bike   ○ ☐ Other
(DRAW YOUR OWN ADVENTURE ICON)

Water body visited on this trip:

○ RIVER/CANAL   ○ LAKE   ○ STREAM   ○ SEA/OCEAN

Who's with me: _____

What's the weather: ☀ ☁ 🌧 🌬☁ ❄

If this nature outing had a badge, it would look like this:

Plants & Insects

Draw some of the plants and bugs you saw on your trip:

What are plants, trees and flowers doing at this time of the year?

Animals

What are animals doing during this time of the year?

Check all types of animals that you saw:

○ BIRD   ○ MAMMAL   ○ FISH

○ AMPHIBIAN   ○ INSECT   ○ REPTILE

Give this trip a name: _____

Place : _____ Date: _____ Season: _____

○ 🧗 **Hike**   ○ 🚲 **Bike**   ○ [ ] **Other**
(DRAW YOUR OWN ADVENTURE ICON)

Water body visited on this trip:

○ RIVER/CANAL   ○ LAKE   ○ STREAM   ○ SEA/OCEAN

Who's with me: _____

What's the weather: ☀   ☁   🌧   🌬   ❄

My sounds, smells and textures collection for this trip:

(LIST OR DRAW ALL THE COOL THINGS YOU HEARD, SMELLED OR TOUCHED ON THIS ADVENTURE)

Top 3 most interesting things I saw on this trip:

Draw some of the plants and insects you saw:

Evidence of animals

DRAW (OR WRITE) WHAT EVIDENCE OF ANIMALS YOU SAW - TRACKS, FOOD, SOUNDS, HOLES, HALF-EATEN ACORNS OR BERRIES...:

Give this trip a name: _____

Place : _____   Date: _____   Season: _____

○ 🧗 **Hike**   ○ 🚲 **Bike**   ○ ☐ **Other**
(DRAW YOUR OWN ADVENTURE ICON)

Water body visited on this trip:

○ RIVER/CANAL   ○ LAKE   ○ STREAM   ○ SEA/OCEAN

Who's with me: _____

What's the weather: ☀ ☁ 🌧 🌬 ❄

If this nature outing had a badge, it would look like this:

Top 3 most interesting things I saw on this trip:

My sounds collection for this outing:

Evidence of animals
DRAW (OR WRITE) WHAT EVIDENCE OF ANIMALS YOU SAW - TRACKS, SOUNDS, HOLES, FOOD (HALF-EATEN ACORNS OR BERRIES...):

Give this trip a name: _____

Place : _____ Date: _____ Season: _____

○ 🧗 Hike   ○ 🚲 Bike   ○ [ ] Other
                                         (DRAW YOUR OWN ADVENTURE ICON)

Water body visited on this trip:

○ RIVER/CANAL   ○ LAKE   ○ STREAM   ○ SEA/OCEAN

Who's with me: _____

What's the weather: ☀   ☁   🌧   🌬   ❄

My sounds, smells and textures collection for this trip:

(LIST OR DRAW ALL THE COOL THINGS YOU HEARD, SMELLED OR TOUCHED ON THIS ADVENTURE)

What is nature doing at this time of the year? What part of their life cycle are plants, insects, birds and other animals in?

Draw the most interesting plants, insects, birds and other animals you saw on this trip:

Give this trip a name: _____

Place : _____ Date: _____ Season: _____

○  Hike

○ Bike

○ [ ] Other
(DRAW YOUR OWN ADVENTURE ICON)

Water body visited on this trip:

○ RIVER/CANAL   ○ LAKE   ○ STREAM   ○ SEA/OCEAN

Who's with me: _____

What's the weather:

If this nature outing had a badge, it would look like this:

Plants & Insects
Draw some of the plants and bugs you saw on your trip:

What are plants, trees and flowers doing at this time of the year?

Animals
What are animals doing during this time of the year?

Check all types of animals that you saw:

- ◯ BIRD
- ◯ MAMMAL
- ◯ FISH
- ◯ AMPHIBIAN
- ◯ INSECT
- ◯ REPTILE

Nature Adventure #8

Give this trip a name: _____

Place : _____ Date: _____ Season: _____

○ 🧗 Hike

○ 🚲 Bike

○ [ ] Other
(DRAW YOUR OWN ADVENTURE ICON)

Water body visited on this trip:

○ RIVER/CANAL   ○ LAKE   ○ STREAM   ○ SEA/OCEAN

Who's with me: _____

What's the weather: ☀ ☁ 🌧 🌬 ❄

My sounds, smells and textures collection for this trip:
(LIST OR DRAW ALL THE COOL THINGS YOU HEARD, SMELLED OR TOUCHED ON THIS ADVENTURE)

Top 3 most interesting things I saw on this trip:

Draw some of the plants and insects you saw:

Evidence of animals

DRAW (OR WRITE) WHAT EVIDENCE OF ANIMALS YOU SAW - TRACKS, FOOD, SOUNDS, HOLES, HALF-EATEN ACORNS OR BERRIES...:

Give this trip a name: _____

Place : _____ Date: _____ Season: _____

○ **Hike**

○ **Bike**

○ **Other**
(DRAW YOUR OWN ADVENTURE ICON)

Water body visited on this trip:
○ RIVER/CANAL   ○ LAKE   ○ STREAM   ○ SEA/OCEAN

Who's with me: _____

What's the weather:

If this nature outing had a badge, it would look like this:

Top 3 most interesting things I saw on this trip:

My sounds collection for this outing:

Evidence of animals
DRAW (OR WRITE) WHAT EVIDENCE OF ANIMALS YOU SAW - TRACKS, SOUNDS, HOLES, FOOD (HALF-EATEN ACORNS OR BERRIES...):

Give this trip a name: _____

Place : _____ Date: _____ Season: _____

○ **Hike**

○ **Bike**

○ **Other**
(DRAW YOUR OWN ADVENTURE ICON)

Water body visited on this trip:

○ RIVER/CANAL   ○ LAKE   ○ STREAM   ○ SEA/OCEAN

Who's with me: _____

What's the weather:

My sounds, smells and textures collection for this trip:
(LIST OR DRAW ALL THE COOL THINGS YOU HEARD, SMELLED OR TOUCHED ON THIS ADVENTURE)

What is nature doing at this time of the year? What part of their life cycle are plants, insects, birds and other animals in?

- -

- -

- -

Draw the most interesting plants, insects, birds and other animals you saw on this trip:

Give this trip a name: ....

Place : .... Date: .... Season: ....

○ 🧗 Hike   ○ 🚲 Bike   ○ [ ] Other
                                        (DRAW YOUR OWN ADVENTURE ICON)

Water body visited on this trip:
○ RIVER/CANAL   ○ LAKE   ○ STREAM   ○ SEA/OCEAN

Who's with me: ....

What's the weather: ☀ ☁ 🌧 🌬 ❄

If this nature outing had a badge, it would look like this:

Plants & Insects
Draw some of the plants and bugs you saw on your trip:

What are plants, trees and flowers doing at this time of the year?

Animals
What are animals doing during this time of the year?

Check all types of animals that you saw:

○ BIRD   ○ MAMMAL   ○ FISH

○ AMPHIBIAN   ○ INSECT   ○ REPTILE

Give this trip a name: ....

Place : .... Date: .... Season: ....

○ **Hike**

○ **Bike**

○ **Other**
(DRAW YOUR OWN ADVENTURE ICON)

Water body visited on this trip:

○ RIVER/CANAL   ○ LAKE   ○ STREAM   ○ SEA/OCEAN

Who's with me: ....

What's the weather:

My sounds, smells and textures collection for this trip:
(LIST OR DRAW ALL THE COOL THINGS YOU HEARD, SMELLED OR TOUCHED ON THIS ADVENTURE)

Top 3 most interesting things I saw on this trip:

Draw some of the plants and insects you saw:

Evidence of animals

DRAW (OR WRITE) WHAT EVIDENCE OF ANIMALS YOU SAW - TRACKS, FOOD, SOUNDS, HOLES, HALF-EATEN ACORNS OR BERRIES...:

Nature Adventure #13

Give this trip a name: _____

Place : _____ Date: _____ Season: _____

○ 🧗 Hike   ○ 🚲 Bike   ○ ☐ Other
                                        (Draw your own adventure icon)

Water body visited on this trip:

○ River/Canal   ○ Lake   ○ Stream   ○ Sea/Ocean

Who's with me: _____

What's the weather: ☀ ☁ 🌧 💨☁ ❄

If this nature outing had a badge, it would look like this:

Top 3 most interesting things I saw on this trip:

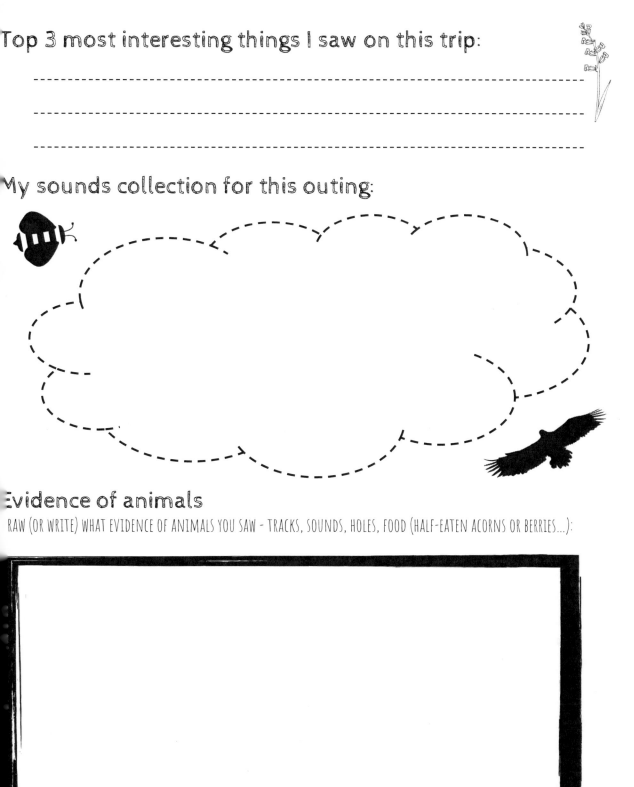

My sounds collection for this outing:

Evidence of animals

RAW (OR WRITE) WHAT EVIDENCE OF ANIMALS YOU SAW - TRACKS, SOUNDS, HOLES, FOOD (HALF-EATEN ACORNS OR BERRIES...):

Nature Adventure #14

Give this trip a name: ....

Place : .... Date: .... Season: ....

○ **Hike**

○ **Bike**

○ **Other**
(DRAW YOUR OWN ADVENTURE ICON)

Water body visited on this trip:

○ RIVER/CANAL   ○ LAKE   ○ STREAM   ○ SEA/OCEAN

Who's with me: ....

What's the weather:

My sounds, smells and textures collection for this trip:
(LIST OR DRAW ALL THE COOL THINGS YOU HEARD, SMELLED OR TOUCHED ON THIS ADVENTURE)

What is nature doing at this time of the year? What part of their life cycle are plants, insects, birds and other animals in?

Draw the most interesting plants, insects, birds and other animals you saw on this trip:

Give this trip a name: --

Place : ------------------------------- Date: ---------- Season: -----------------

○  Hike

○ Bike

○ Other
(DRAW YOUR OWN ADVENTURE ICON)

Water body visited on this trip:

○ RIVER/CANAL   ○ LAKE   ○ STREAM   ○ SEA/OCEAN

Who's with me: --

What's the weather:

If this nature outing had a badge, it would look like this:

Plants & Insects
Draw some of the plants and bugs you saw on your trip:

[drawing box]

What are plants, trees and flowers doing at this time of the year?

Animals
What are animals doing during this time of the year?

Check all types of animals that you saw:

○ BIRD   ○ MAMMAL   ○ FISH

○ AMPHIBIAN   ○ INSECT   ○ REPTILE

Give this trip a name: _____

Place : _____   Date: _____   Season: _____

○ **Hike**

○ **Bike**

○ **Other**
(DRAW YOUR OWN ADVENTURE ICON)

Water body visited on this trip:

○ RIVER/CANAL   ○ LAKE   ○ STREAM   ○ SEA/OCEAN

Who's with me: _____

What's the weather:

My sounds, smells and textures collection for this trip:
(LIST OR DRAW ALL THE COOL THINGS YOU HEARD, SMELLED OR TOUCHED ON THIS ADVENTURE)

Top 3 most interesting things I saw on this trip:

Draw some of the plants and insects you saw:

Evidence of animals

DRAW (OR WRITE) WHAT EVIDENCE OF ANIMALS YOU SAW - TRACKS, FOOD, SOUNDS, HOLES, HALF-EATEN ACORNS OR BERRIES...:

Nature Adventure #17

Give this trip a name: _____

Place : _____ Date: _____ Season: _____

○ 🧗 Hike   ○ 🚲 Bike   ○ ▢ Other
(DRAW YOUR OWN ADVENTURE ICON)

Water body visited on this trip:

○ RIVER/CANAL   ○ LAKE   ○ STREAM   ○ SEA/OCEAN

Who's with me: _____

What's the weather: ☀️ ☁️ 🌧️ 🌬️ ❄️

If this nature outing had a badge, it would look like this:

Top 3 most interesting things I saw on this trip:

My sounds collection for this outing:

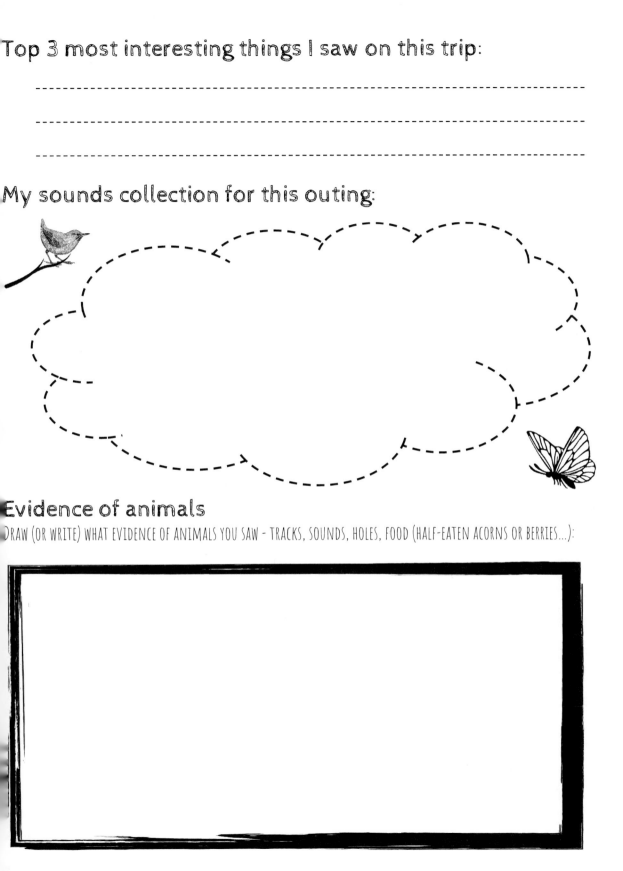

Evidence of animals

Draw (or write) what evidence of animals you saw - tracks, sounds, holes, food (half-eaten acorns or berries...):

Give this trip a name: _____

Place : _____ Date: _____ Season: _____

○ 🧗 Hike   ○ 🚲 Bike   ○ ☐ Other
                                    (DRAW YOUR OWN ADVENTURE ICON)

Water body visited on this trip:

○ RIVER/CANAL   ○ LAKE   ○ STREAM   ○ SEA/OCEAN

Who's with me: _____

What's the weather:

My sounds, smells and textures collection for this trip:
(LIST OR DRAW ALL THE COOL THINGS YOU HEARD, SMELLED OR TOUCHED ON THIS ADVENTURE)

What is nature doing at this time of the year? What part of their life cycle are plants, insects, birds and other animals in?

Draw the most interesting plants, insects, birds and other animals you saw on this trip:

Give this trip a name: _____

Place : _____ Date: _____ Season: _____

○ 🧗 Hike   ○ 🚲 Bike   ○ ☐ Other
(DRAW YOUR OWN ADVENTURE ICON)

Water body visited on this trip:

○ RIVER/CANAL   ○ LAKE   ○ STREAM   ○ SEA/OCEAN

Who's with me: _____

What's the weather: ☀ ☁ 🌧 🌬 ❄

If this nature outing had a badge, it would look like this:

Plants & Insects
Draw some of the plants and bugs you saw on your trip:

What are plants, trees and flowers doing at this time of the year?

Animals
What are animals doing during this time of the year?

Check all types of animals that you saw:

     ◯ BIRD   ◯ MAMMAL   ◯ FISH

     ◯ AMPHIBIAN   ◯ INSECT   ◯ REPTILE

Give this trip a name: _____

Place : _____ Date: _____ Season: _____

◯ 🧗 Hike

◯ 🚴 Bike

◯ ▢ Other
(DRAW YOUR OWN ADVENTURE ICON)

Water body visited on this trip:

◯ RIVER/CANAL   ◯ LAKE   ◯ STREAM   ◯ SEA/OCEAN

Who's with me: _____

What's the weather: ☀ ☁ 🌧 🌬 ❄

My sounds, smells and textures collection for this trip:
(LIST OR DRAW ALL THE COOL THINGS YOU HEARD, SMELLED OR TOUCHED ON THIS ADVENTURE)

Top 3 most interesting things I saw on this trip:

Draw some of the plants and insects you saw:

Evidence of animals

DRAW (OR WRITE) WHAT EVIDENCE OF ANIMALS YOU SAW - TRACKS, FOOD, SOUNDS, HOLES, HALF-EATEN ACORNS OR BERRIES...:

Give this trip a name: _____

Place : _____ Date: _____ Season: _____

○ 🧗 Hike   ○ 🚲 Bike   ○ ☐ Other
(DRAW YOUR OWN ADVENTURE ICON)

Water body visited on this trip:

○ RIVER/CANAL   ○ LAKE   ○ STREAM   ○ SEA/OCEAN

Who's with me: _____

What's the weather: ☀ ☁ 🌧 🌬 ❄

If this nature outing had a badge, it would look like this:

Top 3 most interesting things I saw on this trip:

My sounds collection for this outing:

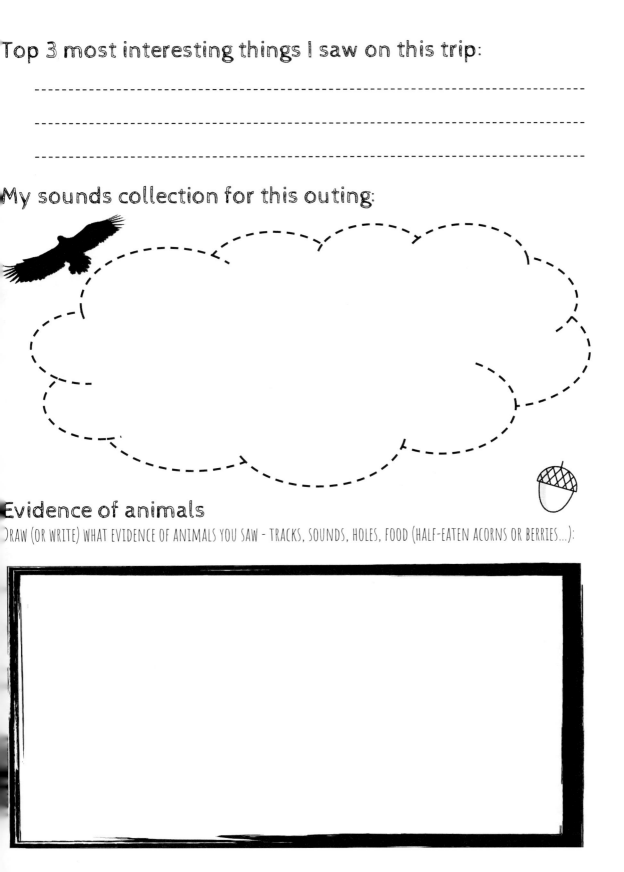

Evidence of animals

DRAW (OR WRITE) WHAT EVIDENCE OF ANIMALS YOU SAW - TRACKS, SOUNDS, HOLES, FOOD (HALF-EATEN ACORNS OR BERRIES...):

Give this trip a name: _____

Place: _____ Date: _____ Season: _____

○ 🧗 Hike

○ 🚲 Bike

○ ⬜ Other
(Draw your own adventure icon)

Water body visited on this trip:

○ River/Canal   ○ Lake   ○ Stream   ○ Sea/Ocean

Who's with me: _____

What's the weather: ☀️ ☁️ 🌧️ 🌬️☁️ ❄️

My sounds, smells and textures collection for this trip:
(List or draw all the cool things you heard, smelled or touched on this adventure)

What is nature doing at this time of the year? What part of their life cycle are plants, insects, birds and other animals in?

Draw the most interesting plants, insects, birds and other animals you saw on this trip:

Give this trip a name: _____

Place : _____ Date: _____ Season: _____

○ 🧗 Hike   ○ 🚲 Bike   ○ ☐ Other
(Draw your own adventure icon)

Water body visited on this trip:

○ River/Canal   ○ Lake   ○ Stream   ○ Sea/Ocean

Who's with me: _____

What's the weather: ☀ ☁ 🌧 🌬 ❄

If this nature outing had a badge, it would look like this:

Plants & Insects

Draw some of the plants and bugs you saw on your trip:

What are plants, trees and flowers doing at this time of the year?

Animals

What are animals doing during this time of the year?

Check all types of animals that you saw:

- ○ Bird
- ○ Amphibian
- ○ Mammal
- ○ Insect
- ○ Fish
- ○ Reptile

Give this trip a name: _____

Place : _____ Date: _____ Season: _____

○ Hike   ○ Bike   ○ [ ] Other
                                                          (DRAW YOUR OWN ADVENTURE ICON)

Water body visited on this trip:
○ RIVER/CANAL   ○ LAKE   ○ STREAM   ○ SEA/OCEAN

Who's with me: _____

What's the weather:

My sounds, smells and textures collection for this trip:
(LIST OR DRAW ALL THE COOL THINGS YOU HEARD, SMELLED OR TOUCHED ON THIS ADVENTURE)

Top 3 most interesting things I saw on this trip:

Draw some of the plants and insects you saw:

Evidence of animals

DRAW (OR WRITE) WHAT EVIDENCE OF ANIMALS YOU SAW - TRACKS, FOOD, SOUNDS, HOLES, HALF-EATEN ACORNS OR BERRIES...:

Give this trip a name: _____

Place : _____ Date: _____ Season: _____

○ **Hike**

○ **Bike**

○ □ **Other**
(DRAW YOUR OWN ADVENTURE ICON)

Water body visited on this trip:

○ RIVER/CANAL   ○ LAKE   ○ STREAM   ○ SEA/OCEAN

Who's with me: _____

What's the weather:

If this nature outing had a badge, it would look like this:

Top 3 most interesting things I saw on this trip:

My sounds collection for this outing:

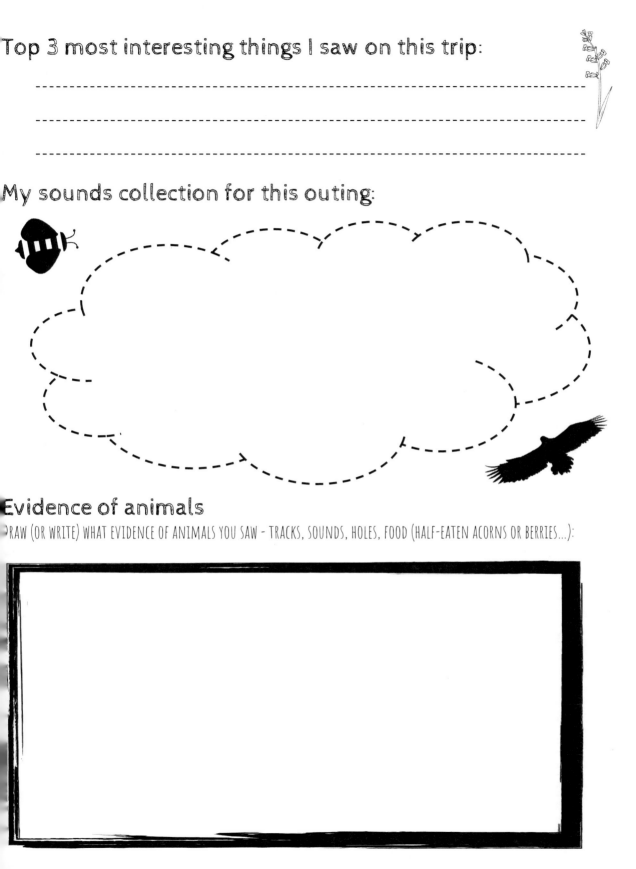

Evidence of animals

DRAW (OR WRITE) WHAT EVIDENCE OF ANIMALS YOU SAW - TRACKS, SOUNDS, HOLES, FOOD (HALF-EATEN ACORNS OR BERRIES...):

Give this trip a name: _____

Place : _____ Date: _____ Season: _____

○ Hike   ○ Bike   ○ [ ] Other
                              (DRAW YOUR OWN ADVENTURE ICON)

Water body visited on this trip:

○ RIVER/CANAL   ○ LAKE   ○ STREAM   ○ SEA/OCEAN

Who's with me: _____

What's the weather:

My sounds, smells and textures collection for this trip:
(LIST OR DRAW ALL THE COOL THINGS YOU HEARD, SMELLED OR TOUCHED ON THIS ADVENTURE)

What is nature doing at this time of the year? What part of their life cycle are plants, insects, birds and other animals in?

Draw the most interesting plants, insects, birds and other animals you saw on this trip:

Give this trip a name: _____

Place: _____ Date: _____ Season: _____

○ 🧗 Hike   ○ 🚲 Bike   ○ ☐ Other
                                      (DRAW YOUR OWN ADVENTURE ICON)

Water body visited on this trip:

○   RIVER/CANAL   ○   LAKE   ○   STREAM   ○   SEA/OCEAN

Who's with me: _____

What's the weather:

If this nature outing had a badge, it would look like this:

Plants & Insects

Draw some of the plants and bugs you saw on your trip:

What are plants, trees and flowers doing at this time of the year?

Animals

What are animals doing during this time of the year?

Check all types of animals that you saw:

- ◯ Bird
- ◯ Mammal
- ◯ Fish
- ◯ Amphibian
- ◯ Insect
- ◯ Reptile

Nature Adventure #28

Give this trip a name: _____

Place : _____ Date: _____ Season: _____

○ 🧗 Hike   ○ 🚲 Bike   ○ ⬜ Other
                                              (DRAW YOUR OWN ADVENTURE ICON)

Water body visited on this trip:

○ RIVER/CANAL   ○ LAKE   ○ STREAM   ○ SEA/OCEAN

Who's with me: _____

What's the weather: ☀️   ☁️   🌧️   🌬️☁️   ❄️

My sounds, smells and textures collection for this trip:

(LIST OR DRAW ALL THE COOL THINGS YOU HEARD, SMELLED OR TOUCHED ON THIS ADVENTURE)

Top 3 most interesting things I saw on this trip:

Draw some of the plants and insects you saw:

Evidence of animals

DRAW (OR WRITE) WHAT EVIDENCE OF ANIMALS YOU SAW - TRACKS, FOOD, SOUNDS, HOLES, HALF-EATEN ACORNS OR BERRIES...:

Give this trip a name: _____

Place : _____ Date: _____ Season: _____

○
Hike

○
Bike

○ ☐
Other
(DRAW YOUR OWN ADVENTURE ICON)

Water body visited on this trip:

○ RIVER/CANAL ○ LAKE ○ STREAM ○ SEA/OCEAN

Who's with me: _____

What's the weather:

If this nature outing had a badge, it would look like this:

Top 3 most interesting things I saw on this trip:

My sounds collection for this outing:

Evidence of animals

DRAW (OR WRITE) WHAT EVIDENCE OF ANIMALS YOU SAW - TRACKS, SOUNDS, HOLES, FOOD (HALF-EATEN ACORNS OR BERRIES...):

Give this trip a name: _____

Place : _____ **Date:** _____ **Season:** _____

○ 🧗 Hike   ○ 🚲 Bike   ○ ☐ Other
(Draw your own adventure icon)

Water body visited on this trip:

○ RIVER/CANAL   ○ LAKE   ○ STREAM   ○ SEA/OCEAN

Who's with me: _____

What's the weather: ☀ ☁ 🌧 🌬☁ ❄

My sounds, smells and textures collection for this trip:
(LIST OR DRAW ALL THE COOL THINGS YOU HEARD, SMELLED OR TOUCHED ON THIS ADVENTURE)

What is nature doing at this time of the year? What part of their life cycle are plants, insects, birds and other animals in?

Draw the most interesting plants, insects, birds and other animals you saw on this trip:

Give this trip a name: _____

Place : _____ Date: _____ Season: _____

○  Hike

○ Bike

○ ⬜ Other
(DRAW YOUR OWN ADVENTURE ICON)

Water body visited on this trip:

○ RIVER/CANAL   ○ LAKE   ○ STREAM   ○ SEA/OCEAN

Who's with me: _____

What's the weather: ☀ ☁ 🌧 💨☁ ❄

If this nature outing had a badge, it would look like this:

Plants & Insects
Draw some of the plants and bugs you saw on your trip:

What are plants, trees and flowers doing at this time of the year?

Animals
What are animals doing during this time of the year?

Check all types of animals that you saw:

○ BIRD   ○ MAMMAL   ○ FISH

○ AMPHIBIAN   ○ INSECT   ○ REPTILE

Give this trip a name: _____

Place : _____ Date: _____ Season: _____

○ 🧗 Hike   ○ 🚲 Bike   ○ ☐ Other
                                         (Draw your own adventure icon)

Water body visited on this trip:
○ River/Canal   ○ Lake   ○ Stream   ○ Sea/Ocean

Who's with me: _____

What's the weather: ☀ ☁ 🌧 🌬 ❄

My sounds, smells and textures collection for this trip:
(List or draw all the cool things you heard, smelled or touched on this adventure)

Top 3 most interesting things I saw on this trip:

Draw some of the plants and insects you saw:

Evidence of animals

DRAW (OR WRITE) WHAT EVIDENCE OF ANIMALS YOU SAW - TRACKS, FOOD, SOUNDS, HOLES, HALF-EATEN ACORNS OR BERRIES...:

Give this trip a name: _____

Place : _____ Date: _____ Season: _____

○ 🧗 Hike   ○ 🚲 Bike   ○ ▢ Other
(DRAW YOUR OWN ADVENTURE ICON)

Water body visited on this trip:

○ RIVER/CANAL   ○ LAKE   ○ STREAM   ○ SEA/OCEAN

Who's with me: _____

What's the weather: ☀ ☁ 🌧 🌬 ❄

If this nature outing had a badge, it would look like this:

Top 3 most interesting things I saw on this trip:

My sounds collection for this outing:

Evidence of animals
DRAW (OR WRITE) WHAT EVIDENCE OF ANIMALS YOU SAW - TRACKS, SOUNDS, HOLES, FOOD (HALF-EATEN ACORNS OR BERRIES...):

Nature Adventure #34

Give this trip a name: _____

Place : _____ Date: _____ Season: _____

○ 🧗 Hike

○ 🚲 Bike

○ [ ] Other
(DRAW YOUR OWN ADVENTURE ICON)

Water body visited on this trip:

○ RIVER/CANAL   ○ LAKE   ○ STREAM   ○ SEA/OCEAN

Who's with me: _____

What's the weather:

My sounds, smells and textures collection for this trip:
(LIST OR DRAW ALL THE COOL THINGS YOU HEARD, SMELLED OR TOUCHED ON THIS ADVENTURE)

What is nature doing at this time of the year? What part of their life cycle are plants, insects, birds and other animals in?

Draw the most interesting plants, insects, birds and other animals you saw on this trip:

Give this trip a name: _____

Place : _____ Date: _____ Season: _____

○ 🧗 Hike   ○ 🚲 Bike   ○ ☐
                                        Other
                                   (DRAW YOUR OWN ADVENTURE ICON)

Water body visited on this trip:

○   RIVER/CANAL   ○   LAKE   ○   STREAM   ○   SEA/OCEAN

Who's with me: _____

What's the weather: ☀   ☁   🌧   🌬☁   ❄

If this nature outing had a badge, it would look like this:

Plants & Insects
Draw some of the plants and bugs you saw on your trip:

What are plants, trees and flowers doing at this time of the year?

Animals
What are animals doing during this time of the year?

Check all types of animals that you saw:

○ BIRD   ○ MAMMAL   ○ FISH

○ AMPHIBIAN   ○ INSECT   ○ REPTILE

Give this trip a name: _____

Place : _____ **Date:** _____ **Season:** _____

○ 🧗 Hike   ○ 🚲 Bike   ○ ☐ Other
(Draw your own adventure icon)

Water body visited on this trip:

○ River/Canal   ○ Lake   ○ Stream   ○ Sea/Ocean

Who's with me: _____

What's the weather: ☀ ☁ 🌧 🌬☁ ❄

My sounds, smells and textures collection for this trip:
(List or draw all the cool things you heard, smelled or touched on this adventure)

Top 3 most interesting things I saw on this trip:

Draw some of the plants and insects you saw:

Evidence of animals

DRAW (OR WRITE) WHAT EVIDENCE OF ANIMALS YOU SAW - TRACKS, FOOD, SOUNDS, HOLES, HALF-EATEN ACORNS OR BERRIES...:

Nature Adventure #37

Give this trip a name: _____

Place : _____ Date: _____ Season: _____

○ 🧗 Hike   ○ 🚲 Bike   ○ [ ] Other
                                        (DRAW YOUR OWN ADVENTURE ICON)

Water body visited on this trip:

○ RIVER/CANAL   ○ LAKE   ○ STREAM   ○ SEA/OCEAN

Who's with me: _____

What's the weather: ☀️ ☁️ 🌧️ 🌬️☁️ ❄️

If this nature outing had a badge, it would look like this:

Top 3 most interesting things I saw on this trip:

My sounds collection for this outing:

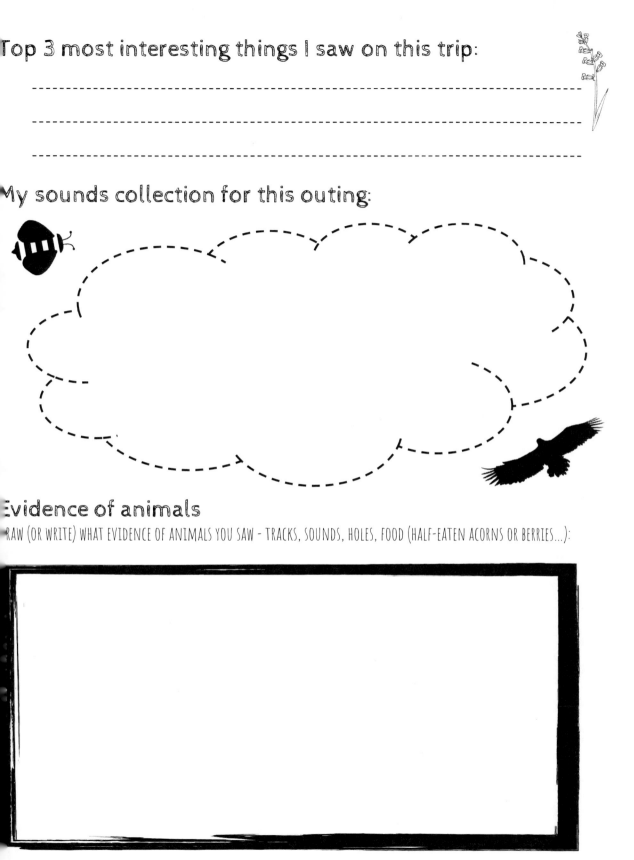

Evidence of animals

DRAW (OR WRITE) WHAT EVIDENCE OF ANIMALS YOU SAW - TRACKS, SOUNDS, HOLES, FOOD (HALF-EATEN ACORNS OR BERRIES...):

Give this trip a name: _____

Place : _____ Date: _____ Season: _____

◯ 🧗 Hike   ◯ 🚲 Bike   ◯ ☐ Other
(Draw your own adventure icon)

Water body visited on this trip:

◯ River/Canal   ◯ Lake   ◯ Stream   ◯ Sea/Ocean

Who's with me: _____

What's the weather: ☀ ☁ 🌧 🌬☁ ❄

My sounds, smells and textures collection for this trip:
(List or draw all the cool things you heard, smelled or touched on this adventure)

What is nature doing at this time of the year? What part of their life cycle are plants, insects, birds and other animals in?

Draw the most interesting plants, insects, birds and other animals you saw on this trip:

Give this trip a name: _____

Place : _____ Date: _____ Season: _____

○ 🧗 Hike   ○ 🚲 Bike   ○ ☐ Other
                                          (DRAW YOUR OWN ADVENTURE ICON)

Water body visited on this trip:

○ RIVER/CANAL   ○ LAKE   ○ STREAM   ○ SEA/OCEAN

Who's with me: _____

What's the weather: ☀ ☁ 🌧 🌬 ❄

If this nature outing had a badge, it would look like this:

Plants & Insects

Draw some of the plants and bugs you saw on your trip:

What are plants, trees and flowers doing at this time of the year?

Animals

What are animals doing during this time of the year?

Check all types of animals that you saw:

- ◯ BIRD
- ◯ MAMMAL
- ◯ FISH
- ◯ AMPHIBIAN
- ◯ INSECT
- ◯ REPTILE

Give this trip a name: _____

Place : _____ Date: _____ Season: _____

○ Hike   ○ Bike   ○ [ ] Other
(Draw your own adventure icon)

Water body visited on this trip:

○ River/Canal   ○ Lake   ○ Stream   ○ Sea/Ocean

Who's with me: _____

What's the weather:

My sounds, smells and textures collection for this trip:
(List or draw all the cool things you heard, smelled or touched on this adventure)

Top 3 most interesting things I saw on this trip:

Draw some of the plants and insects you saw:

Evidence of animals

DRAW (OR WRITE) WHAT EVIDENCE OF ANIMALS YOU SAW - TRACKS, FOOD, SOUNDS, HOLES, HALF-EATEN ACORNS OR BERRIES...:

What has been your absolutely most favorite nature adventure so far?
Describe and draw what you loved about it:
